D1515146

WITHDRAWN

048925

WINDSOR PARK
BOYS' & GIRLS' DEPT.

For Roger

Copyright © 1989 by Bennett, Jill, Rees, Mary

All rights reserved. No part of this publication may be reproduced or transmitted in any form or by any means, electronic or mechanical, including photocopy, recording, or any information storage or retrieval system without permission in writing from the publisher.

Published in 1989 by
Stoddart Publishing Co. Limited
34 Lesmill Road
Toronto, Canada
M3B 2T6

Published in Great Britain
Heinemann Young Books
Michelin House
81 Fulham Road
London SW3 6RB

Canadian Cataloguing in Publication Data

Main entry under title:

Spooky poems

ISBN 0–7737–2350–1

1. Children's poetry, English. 2. Children's poetry, American. I. Bennett, Jill. II. Rees, Mary, 1960–

PR1175, S66 1989   821′.008′09282   C89-094094-0

Produced by Mandarin Offset
Printed and bound in Hong Kong

WINNIPEG
JAN 11 1991
PUBLIC LIBRARY

Spooky Poems

Collected by Jill Bennett

Pictures by Mary Rees

Stoddart

THE SPANGLED PANDEMONIUM

The Spangled Pandemonium
Is missing from the zoo.
He bent the bars the barest bit,
And slithered glibly through.

He crawled across the moated wall,
He climbed the mango tree,
And when his keeper scrambled up,
He nipped him in the knee.

To all of you, a warning
Not to wander after dark,
Or if you must, make very sure
You stay out of the park.

For the Spangled Pandemonium
Is missing from the zoo,
And since he nipped his keeper,
He would just as soon nip you!

Palmer Brown

048925
WINDSOR PARK
BOYS' & GIRLS' DEPT.

THE HAIRY TOE

Once there was a woman went out to pick beans,
and she found a Hairy Toe.
She took the Hairy Toe home with her,
and that night, when she went to bed,
the wind began to moan and groan.
Away off in the distance
she seemed to hear a voice crying,
"Who's got my Hair-r-ry To-o-oe?
Who's got my Hair-r-ry To-o-oe?"

The woman scrooched down,
'way down under the covers,
and about that time
the wind appeared to hit the house,
smoosh,
and the old house creaked and cracked
like something was trying to get in.
The voice had come nearer,
almost at the door now,
and it said,
"Where's my Hair-r-ry To-o-oe?
Who's got my Hair-r-ry To-o-oe?"

The woman scrooched further down
under the covers
and pulled them tight around her head.

The wind growled around the house
like some big animal
and r-r-um-mbled
over the chimbley.
All at once she heard the door cr-r-a-ack
and Something slipped in
and began to creep over the floor.

The floor went
cre-e-eak, cre-e-eak
at every step that thing took towards her bed.
The woman could almost feel
it bending over her bed.
Then in an awful voice it said:
"Where's my Hair-r-ry To-o-oe?
Who's got my Hair-r-ry To-o-oe?"

You've got it!"

trad. American

THE BAT

The bat in flight at dead of night
Can flap about with ease,
For with his ears he somehow steers
A path between the trees.

Colin West

THE TWITCHETTY WITCH

A Twitchetty Witch
Went hurtling by,
Twitchetty, Witchetty,
Yooo-hooo-hooo!
Up in the dark
Where the black bats fly,
With her pointed nose
And her glittering eye,
A Twitchetty Witch
Went hurtling by,
Twitchetty, Witchetty –
S-w-w-i-i-i-s-shh!

Lilian Boucher

THE ALPHABET MONSTER

I'm the Alphabet Monster
And nothing tastes better
To the Alphabet Monster
Than eating a letter.
A "j" and an "a"
And a "c" and a "k"
And the million more letters
I munch every day.

I'm hungry now.
What shall I do?
I think I'll eat
a "y"
an "o"
and a "u"

That means . . . YOU!

Robert Heidbreder

HAUNTED HOUSE

There's a house upon the hilltop
We will not go inside
For that is where the witches live,
Where ghosts and goblins hide.

Tonight they have their party,
All the lights are burning bright,
But oh we will not go inside
The haunted house tonight.

The demons there are whirling
And the spirits swirl about.
They sing their songs to Hallowe'en.
"Come join the fun," they shout.

But we do not want to go there
So we run with all our might
And oh we will not go inside
The haunted house tonight.

Jack Prelutsky

THE SLITHEREE-DEE

The Slitheree-dee has crawled out of the sea;
He may catch all the others, but he won't catch me.
No, you won't catch me, old Slitheree-dee;
You may catch all the others, but you wo . . .

Shel Silverstein

MY OTHER GRANNY

My Granny is an Octopus
At the bottom of the sea,
And when she comes to supper
She brings her family.

She chooses a wild wet windy night
When the world rolls blind
As a boulder in the night-sea surf,
And her family troops behind.

Ted Hughes

I LEFT MY HEAD

I left my head
somewhere
today.

Put it down for
just
a minute.

Under the
table?
On a chair?

Wish I were
able
to say
where.

Everything I need
is
in it!

Lilian Moore

THE HIDEBEHIND

Have you seen the Hidebehind?
I don't think you will, mind you,
because as you're running through the dark
the Hidebehind's behind you.

Michael Rosen

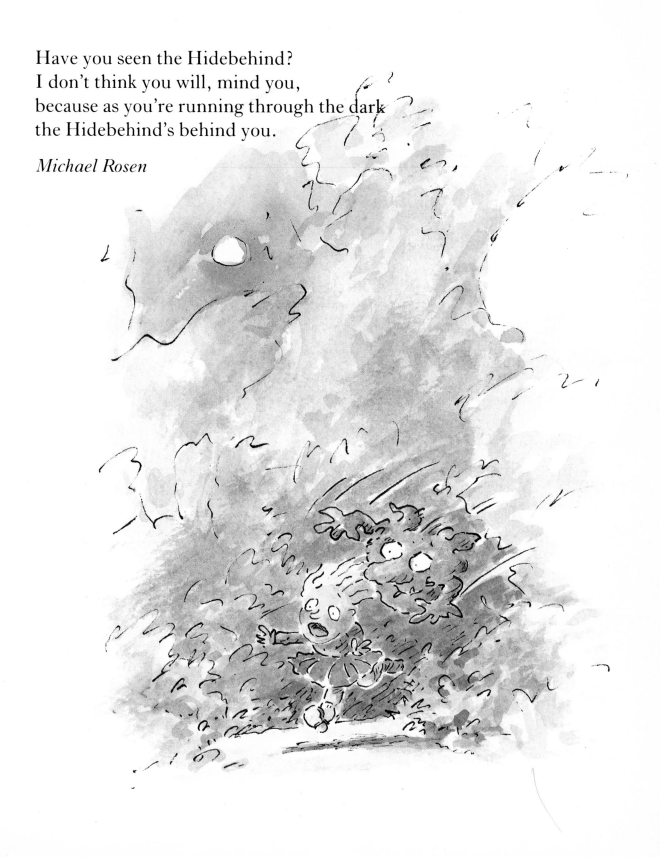

THE UGSTABUGGLE

Over by my bedroom wall
The Ugstabuggle stands,
A monster nearly nine feet tall
With hairy, grasping hands.
In afternoons and mornings
He's always out of sight,
But often I can see him
In the darkness late at night.
Yet when I do not think of him
He disappears again,
And when I sleep he goes, because
I cannot see him then!

Peter Wesley-Smith

THE MARROG

My desk's at the back of the class
And nobody, nobody knows
I'm a Marrog from Mars
With a body of brass
And seventeen fingers and toes.

Wouldn't they shriek if they knew
I've three eyes at the back of my head
And my hair is bright purple
My nose is deep blue
And my teeth are half-yellow, half-red

My five arms are silver, and spiked
With knives on them sharper than spears.
I could go back right now, if I liked—
And return in a million light-years.

I could gobble them all,
For I'm seven foot tall
And I'm breathing green flames from my ears.

Wouldn't they yell if they knew,
If they guessed that a Marrog was here?
Ha-ha, they haven't a clue—
Or wouldn't they tremble with fear!
"Look, look, a Marrog"
They'd all scream—and SMACK
The blackboard would fall and the ceiling would crack

And teacher would faint, I suppose.
But I grin to myself, sitting right at the back
And nobody, nobody knows.

R. C. Scriven

MONSTER

I saw a monster in the woods
As I was cycling by,
His footsteps smouldered in the leaves,
His breath made bushes die,

And when he raised his hairy arm
It blotted out the sun;
He snatched a pigeon from the sky
And swallowed it in one.

His mouth was like a dripping cave,
His eyes like pools of lead,
And when he growled I rode back home
And rushed upstairs to bed.

But that was yesterday and though
It gave me quite a fright,
I'm older now and braver so
I'm going back tonight.

I'll tie him up when he's asleep
And take him to the zoo.
The trouble is he's rather big . . .
Will you come too?

Richard Edwards

SOMETHING IS THERE

Something is there
there on the stair
coming down
    coming down
        stepping with care.
Coming down
    coming down
        slinkety-sly.

Something is coming and wants to get by.

Lilian Moore

I'M ALONE IN THE EVENING

I'm alone in the evening
when the family sits
reading and sleeping
and I watch the fire in close
to see flame goblins
wriggling out of their caves
for the evening

I'm alone

when mum's switched out the light
my head against the pillow
listening to a ca-thump ca-thump
in the middle of my ears.
It's my heart.

Michael Rosen

THE BAD DREAM

Sleep . . . deep.
Night . . . FRIGHT!
Dream . . . SCREAM!
Mum . . . comes.
"There, there . . ."
Kiss, kiss . . .
Thumb . . . mmmmm.
"Night, night . . .
Sleep tight . . ."
Sleep . . . deep . . .

Tony Bradman

hist   whist
little ghostthings
tip-toe
twinkle toe

little twitchy
witches and tingling
goblins
hob-a-nob

hob-a-nob

little hoppy happy
toad in tweeds
tweeds
little itchy mousies

with scuttling
eyes   rustle and run and
hidehidehide
whisk

whisk   look out for the old woman
with the wart on her nose
what she'll do to yer
nobody knows

for she knows the devil   ooch
the devil   ouch
the devil
ach   the great

green
dancing
devil
devil

devil
devil

wheeEEE

e. e. cummings

OUR POND

The pond in our garden
Is murky and deep
And lots of things live there
That slither and creep.

Like diving bell spiders
And great ramshorn snails
And whirligig beetles
And black snappertails.

There used to be goldfish
That nibbled my thumb,
But now there's just algae
And sour, crusty scum.

There used to be pondweed
With fizzy green shoots,
But now there are leeches
And horrible newts.

One day when my football
Rolled in by mistake
I tried to retrieve it
By using a rake,

But as I leaned over
A shape from the ooze
Bulged up like a nightmare
And lunged at my shoes.

I ran back in shouting.
But everyone laughed
And said I was teasing
Or else I was daft.

But I know what happened
And when I'm asleep
I dream of those creatures
That slither and creep.

Richard Edwards

THE GOBLIN

There's a goblin as green
As a goblin can be
Who is sitting outside
And is waiting for me.
When he knocked on my door
And said softly, "Come play!"
I answered, "No thank you,
Now please, go away!"
But the goblin as green
As a goblin can be
Is still sitting outside
And is waiting for me.

Jack Prelutsky

GHOST

I saw a ghost
that stared and stared
And I stood still
and acted scared.

But that was just
a big pretend.

I knew that ghost . . .

. . . it was my friend!

Jack Prelutsky

THE SMALL GHOSTIE

When it's late and it's dark
And everyone sleeps . . . shhh shhh shhh,
Into our kitchen
A small ghostie creeps . . . shhh shhh shhh.

We hear knockings and raps
And then rattles and taps,

Then he clatters and clangs
And he batters and bangs,

And he whistles and yowls
And he screeches and howls . . .

So we pull up our covers over our heads
And we block up our ears and WE STAY IN OUR BEDS.

Barbara Ireson

CHEEKY LITTLE SKELETON

I was sitting in the bath one day
when in walked a skeleton.
He hadn't any clothes on
but he wore a pair of wellingtons.
I looked at him and he looked at me,
he said, I'm coming in to get you.
One, two, three.

He dived into the bath with me,
I couldn't stand the sight of him.
I knew that I was trapped so
I agreed to fight with him.
He hadn't any muscles and he wasn't very strong,
pulling him to pieces
didn't take me very long.

As I stepped out of the bath,
he began to speak to me.
If I put him back together
there'd be a special treat for me.
Put me back together, boy, and watch me disappear.
He looked awfully untidy,
bones were lying everywhere.

So I put him back together,
that cheeky little skeleton.
As quiet as a mouse he sat,
as I slipped on his wellingtons.
I looked at him and he looked at me,
he said, I'm gonna have to leave you, boy,
One, two, three.

And he disappeared.

Lorraine Simeon

WHAT'S THAT?

What's that?
Who's there?
There's a great huge horrible *horrible*
creeping up the stair!
A huge big terrible *terrible*
with creepy crawly hair!
There's a ghastly grisly *ghastly*
with seven slimy eyes!
And flabby grabby tentacles
of a gigantic size!
He's crept into my room now,
he's leaning over me.
I wonder if he's thinking
how delicious I will be.

Florence Parry Heide

I know a man
Who's back to front
The strangest man *I've* seen.
He can't tell where he's going
But he knows where he has been.

Spike Milligan

The Witch! the Witch! don't let her get you!

Or your Aunt wouldn't know you the next time
she met you!

Eleanor Farjeon